The Visual Gu

Asperger's Syndrome: Helping Siblings

by Alis Rowe

Also by Alis Rowe

One Lonely Mind
978-0-9562693-0-0

The Girl with the Curly Hair - Asperger's and Me
978-0-9562693-2-4

The 1st Comic Book
978-0-9562693-1-7

The 2nd Comic Book
978-0-95626934-8

The 3rd Comic Book
978-0-9562693-3-1

The 4th Comic Book
978-15086839-7-1

Websites:
www.thegirlwiththecurlyhair.co.uk

Social Media:
www.facebook.com/thegirlwiththecurlyhair
www.twitter.com/curlyhairedalis

The Visual Guide to

Asperger's Syndrome: Helping Siblings

by Alis Rowe

Lonely Mind Books
London

For parents and siblings of children with ASD

hello

Children are all unique. It's a given that the child with Autism Spectrum Disorder (ASD) will have special needs but families must also consider the needs of their non-ASD (NT) child.

Having a child with ASD can be very stressful at times, not just for the parents, but for the sibling(s) too.

This book provides insight and guidance for parents to help talk to their child or children about the sibling with ASD.

I hope you enjoy this book

Alis aka The Girl with the Curly Hair

Contents

Explaining ASD

Autism Spectrum Disorder (ASD) is bit like eye colour - you just have it! And it will be with you forever

Different things are stressful when you have ASD, but with understanding and help from the child's parents and from siblings, everyone in the family can feel happy and fulfilled

Although ASD is thought to be a genetic condition, it can't be "caught" like the common cold... so it's not contagious

There are a few things that are really important for the neurotypical (NT) sibling to know, for example:

THE WAY SHE ACTS IS NOT MY FAULT. I THOUGHT I WAS DOING THINGS TO CAUSE HER BEHAVIOUR

SOME OF THE THINGS SHE DOES, SHE DOESN'T DO ON PURPOSE

SHE REPEATS THINGS BECAUSE SHE'S TRYING TO UNDERSTAND. SHE ASKS "WHY?" BECAUSE SHE DOESN'T UNDERSTAND

MY SISTER IS NOT THE ONLY ONE WHO HAS ASD. LOTS OF PEOPLE HAVE IT AND THEY CAN HAVE HAPPY, SUCCESSFUL LIVES!

Teaching your children from a young age about how everyone is different and that there is no one, single 'correct' way to be is a very important step in helping them become empathetic individuals

Making sure children know that there are lots of positives to being different is a helpful discussion to have, for example think about the benefits of being:

a very tall person

a very quiet person

a person with very good attention to detail

a person with a very good sense of smell

a person with a single, very intense hobby

Having a child with ASD can be stressful. As a parent, it may feel as though you give them all your attention and your neurotypical child may feel they're second best

Your child with ASD will be a central figure in your neurotypical child's life

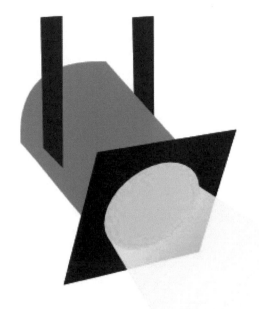

How your NT child may feel about their ASD sibling

Unfortunately, your NT child may have negative feelings because of their autistic sibling

The accumulation of these feelings over a long period of time can lead to your NT child feeling resentment towards their brother or sister

SHE SEEMS TO GET AWAY WITH THINGS THAT I DON'T GET AWAY WITH. IT'S NOT FAIR

SOME OF HER BEHAVIOURS ARE VERY ODD. I FEEL EMBARRASSED HAVING FRIENDS ROUND OR BEING OUT WITH HER

SHE DOESN'T GET TOLD OFF WHEN SHE'S BEING NAUGHTY. IT'S NOT FAIR

ANY LITTLE THING CAN CAUSE HER TO HAVE 'MELTDOWNS.' I WORRY ABOUT SAYING OR DOING THE WRONG THING IN CASE I SET HER OFF. IT'S EASIER TO STAY AWAY FROM HER

I DON'T UNDERSTAND WHY SHE WON'T PLAY WITH ME LIKE MY FRIENDS' SISTERS PLAY WITH THEM. DOES SHE NOT LIKE ME? I FEEL SAD, FRUSTRATED AND CONFUSED

SHE GETS A LOT MORE ATTENTION THAN I DO. IT FEELS AS THOUGH SHE'S 'THE FAVOURITE'

SHE OFTEN JUST COMPLETELY IGNORES ME WHEN I'M TALKING TO HER. IT MAKES ME FEEL ANGRY

SHE DOESN'T CARE HOW I FEEL. SHE IS SELFISH

It might be helpful to break down each worry into 1) an explanation and 2) a solution

Let's look at some examples

"She doesn't get told off when she's being naughty"

Explanation	Solution
•"Your sibling doesn't realise when he or she has done something wrong. We have to teach them" •"It takes him or her a long time to learn certain things" •"You can tell us when he or she has done something naughty and we will resolve it"	•Have patience and be clear •Communicate with your ASD child about what they have done wrong and why •Reassure your NT child that you are aware of the ASD sibling's behaviour and that you are trying to resolve the problem, even though it might take a long time for their behaviour to change •Keep checking in with your NT child so they know their views and feelings are being taken seriously

"She won't play with me"

Explanation	Solution
•The ASD child may not understand what the NT child is wanting them to do and feel confused •The ASD child has different hobbies to their NT sibling •The ASD child plays in a different way, e.g. wants to 'control' the game, won't be very imaginative, or wants to strictly follow the rules •The ASD child needs much more Alone Time than their NT sibling	•Be clear about what the rules of the game are and what the ASD child is expected to do •Board games, video games or sports may be a better solution than imaginative child play •Think about other activities the children could do together instead, such as going cycling or playing tennis •Lego® Therapy* can be fun for all the family •When the ASD child needs time to be on their own, let them have some space •Ensure the NT child spends plenty of time with their friends or participates in extra-curricular social activities

*Simon Baron-Cohen (2014). Lego® - Based Therapy: How to Build Social Competence Through Lego®-Based Clubs for Children with Autism and Related Conditions. London: Jessica Kingsley Publishers.

"She ignores me when I'm talking to her"

Explanation	Solution
•"Your brother or sister may not realise you are talking to them unless you say their name" •"They may not understand what you are saying" •"They may be distracted by the noise and light around them" •"They may need to finish what they are doing first, before they will talk with you"	•Get your ASD child's attention before talking to them, for example, by saying their name •Check what the environment is like, e.g. is the washing machine on? Is the TV on? Are there lots of other people in the room? A sensory stimulating environment can be distracting •Make sure that they have finished what they are doing before conversing with them or ask to speak to them at a certain time •Speak very clearly and say exactly what you mean

"She doesn't care how I feel"

Explanation	Solution
•"Your brother or sister finds it hard to understand that other people have different thoughts and feelings from them. This is part of his or her ASD" •"He or she may find it hard to show or tell you how they are feeling" •"He or she may know you're upset but not know what to do. We need to tell he or she what you would like them to do" •"He or she may not realise that you're upset. We need to tell him or her how we feel very clearly and why"	•The NT child can learn to very clearly say how they feel and why, instead of assuming the ASD child will intuitively know •The ASD child needs to learn why their behaviour might have upset their brother or sister •Schedule "family meetings" once a week to discuss the week's events together •Teach your ASD child about how other people might see the world using stories, TV programmes, films, etc. •Have signs to represent emotions, e.g. your NT child could hold up an emotion card saying 'sad' (your children could make these cards together) •The ASD child needs to learn what they can do when their sibling feels a particular way, in order to help them (often it's just learning to ask their sibling what would help)

"She gets all the attention"

Explanation	Solution
•"Your brother or sister needs more help with some things you find easy, like getting dressed or getting ready for school" •"Sometimes you need help with different things and that's when we help you"	•Timetable in daily individual time with each of your children, even 10 minutes a day makes a big difference •Help your ASD child to become more independent •Do not mollycoddle your ASD child •Show interest in your NT child's hobbies

Ways to support your NT child

It is common for your NT child to feel guilty that they have friends and their ASD sibling does not

An approach to this problem might include:

- Helping your NT child to include their ASD sibling in more structured activities with their friends, such as board games, drawing, sport, watching a film
- It might help if their ASD sibling explains that they like to be introduced to the friends but not forced to join in as they actually like spending time on their own
- Remember that often the ASD child might prefer not to be disturbed and prefer their own

routine

- Your NT child needs to understand that they enjoy different things and their ASD sibling may not feel they are missing out by not participating

Very often, your NT child will have very little time on their own with you

An approach to this problem might include:

- Scheduling special time with your NT child on a regular basis, where they are the focus of attention, not their ASD brother or sister
- Time with your NT child can be scheduled to fit the family routine, for example: A 10 minute activity before bed each night, an hour every other evening, Saturday afternoons, a day out once a month
- Try to arrange that your NT child has some time in the house with you when their ASD sibling isn't there

- Encourage your NT child to involve you in their hobbies

Your NT child can feel restricted by the routines that their ASD sibling follows

An approach to this problem might include:

• Having film or game days where different family members get to take turns in choosing what to watch or what game to play
• Make sure you don't miss out on the things that are important to your NT child, such as a school recital, a play or a sports match. Consider childcare so that one or both of you can attend the event
• If events are likely to get cut short because your ASD child cannot manage, make sure your NT child can still enjoy their favourite parts by, for

example, doing the activities that they like first, or allowing them to stay later while the ASD child is taken home or has a break

Your NT child can feel embarrassed by their ASD sibling or feels guilty for feeling embarrassed

An approach to this problem might include:

- Letting your NT child know that you understand and that it's OK to feel embarrassed
- If your NT child feels comfortable, you should equip them with enough information and confidence to talk about their sibling's ASD to other people. Prepare them for these kinds of conversations and help them come up with simple, efficient explanations for their peers, which might make things easier for them in the

long run
- You should emphasise that there will always be some people who don't understand

Helping the ASD child become more independent

Learning to help around the house is a very important life skill

Parents should not underestimate the ability of their ASD child - there will always be something they can do

Not doing any chores can lead to resentment from the NT sibling

As the NT sibling gets older, he or she will understand and accept any accommodations for their ASD brother or sister the parents have to make

I AM GOOD AT LAYING THE TABLE AND FOLDING NAPKINS

I LIKE THE REPETITIVE NATURE OF USING THE VACUUM CLEANER. I LIKE SEEING HOW CLEAN THE CARPET GETS. I WEAR EARPLUGS TO COPE WITH THE NOISE

I ENJOY BRUSHING THE CATS AND TAKING THE DOG FOR A WALK. I LIKE CARING FOR OUR PETS

AS LONG AS I AM SHOWN EXACTLY WHAT I NEED TO DO, I AM GOOD AT CLEANING THE SHOWER AND SINK

I DON'T MIND TAKING CLEAN DISHES AND CUTLERY OUT OF THE DISHWASHER. I CAN PUT THEM AWAY NEATLY IN THE RIGHT PLACES. MY HANDS DON'T GET DIRTY

I CAN HELP PUT THE SHOPPING AWAY BECAUSE I CAN PUT ALL THE ITEMS IN A NICE ORDER

Often the three reasons that chores are not done by the ASD child are to do with communication:

1) the task is not specific enough

2) they do not know how to do it

3) they do not realise that the task needs to be done

Example of the task not being specific enough:

Dad says something to The Girl with the Curly Hair

In this example, Dad is just making a statement

The Girl with the Curly Hair takes what he has said to literally just mean that the house is a mess

Perhaps it would have been better for Dad to have very clearly stated what he meant by "a mess" (e.g. "The carpet in the hall is very dirty") and to very clearly state what he wanted her to do (e.g. "Please would you vacuum the hall today?")

The Girl with the Curly Hair then would have done it!

Example of not knowing how to do a task:

Dad says something to The Girl with the Curly Hair

Even though cleaning the shower is a very obvious and simple task to Dad, it is not obvious or simple to The Girl with the Curly Hair

She would find it very helpful if he very clearly told and showed her exactly what to do, as well as if he made suggestions on exactly how often it needed to be cleaned or what the signs were that it needs cleaning

This requires patience from Dad, who needs to recognise that although this task is simple to him, it's not to her

Then she would do it!

Example of not realising a task needs to be done:

Dad says something to The Girl with the Curly Hair

A lot of the time people see things in different ways, for example Dad saw the bushes as being overgrown whereas The Girl with the Curly Hair thought they were lovely

If he has a preference for how the bushes ought to look, then he needs to very clearly explain this to her so that she knows to monitor how overgrown the garden is. He needs to explain to her what signs to look out for that signal the garden has become overgrown

She'll then start doing the pruning!

Hypersensitivities

Neurotypical people generally have balanced, comfortable senses. To be told their ASD brother or sister is "over sensitive" to sensations can be meaningless

Think about some ways you could relate senses to senses that they find uncomfortable, for example:

Description of sense ASD child finds uncomfortable	How to relate it to something an NT child can understand
"Sounds can be sharp, loud and painful...	...like that feeling you get when you hear fingernails on a chalk board!"
"Touch can be very painful...	...like how you feel when you bang your head or when you have to comb out a knot in your hair"
"Smells can be nauseating...	...like how you feel when you smell milk that has gone off!"
"Light can be so bright...	...that it feels like your eyes are burning. Think about how you feel when the Optician shines lights right in your eyes"

This might help your NT child develop more empathy when they are doing something that might cause significant sensory discomfort to their ASD brother or sister

It might be helpful to think about how to be more considerate of the ASD child's sensory needs, for example the NT child could listen to their loud music through headphones or they could eat strong-smelling food in another room

The ASD child also needs to learn what they can do for themselves to get away from an uncomfortable sensation, such as putting earplugs in or going to their room

Of course it is important for the NT child to be considerate of their ASD sibling's sensory challenges, however it is very important for the ASD child to learn what they can do themselves when there are uncomfortable sensations around, as this will teach them independence and tolerance for living in the outside world

Attention to detail

Small details might be very apparent to your ASD child

Whilst your NT child might find this frustrating when for example imperfections in their work are pointed out, it is equally frustrating for your ASD child when they see the imperfections... they feel they have to point them out and may think they are being helpful in doing so

For example, when your NT child shows you their story, feeling very proud of their work, they may feel hurt and angry when their ASD brother or sister points out a missing apostrophe...

Once upon a
time there was
a Prince. The
Princes name
was Jack.

Parents could say "apostrophes are such tricky things! Thanks for pointing that out. The story is really interesting and a lot of work has gone into it. We are so proud of you both"

Meltdowns

The Volcano Theory

Meltdowns are outbursts that might occur when your ASD child feels anxious or overwhelmed

It might be helpful to explain to your NT child that meltdowns are like volcanoes

They may sometimes seem very quick and abrupt, but they may also simmer for hours and erupt at a later time

The Bucket Theory

Another helpful way to explain meltdowns is that they occur when the ASD child's 'bucket' gets full

This bucket can be full of things such as anxiety or sensory discomfort and can get fuller and fuller throughout the day until eventually it overflows (and this is when the meltdown occurs)

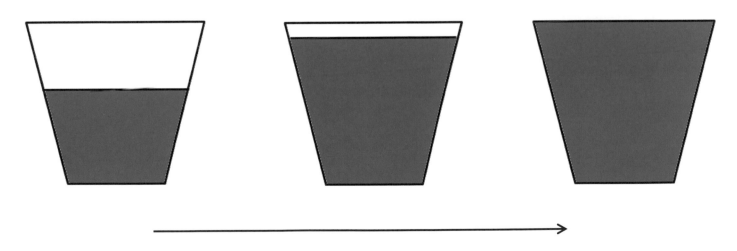

'bucket' getting more full as the day goes on

A meltdown might look similar to a temper tantrum

It is important to explain to the NT child that, although they are similar, a meltdown is different from a tantrum and your ASD child will find it extremely difficult to stop it, as a meltdown is usually driven by anxiety, rather than frustration or anger

Help your NT child to understand that their brother or sister having a meltdown is not just them trying to get their own way, they are probably extremely stressed and anxious

The Filter Theory

Whereas neurotypical people have filters that enable them to enjoy or cope with everyday situations, autistic people might not have this filter

This can cause the bucket to overflow

This may be your NT child's experience of lunch in the dinner hall at school:

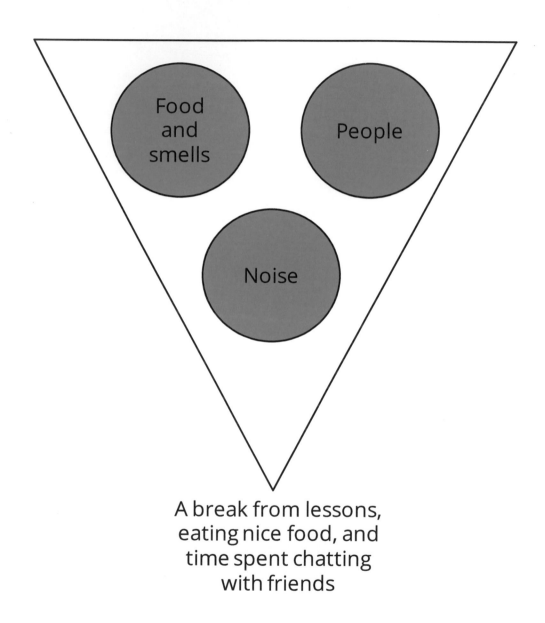

This is their ASD sibling's experience of lunch in the dinner hall at school:

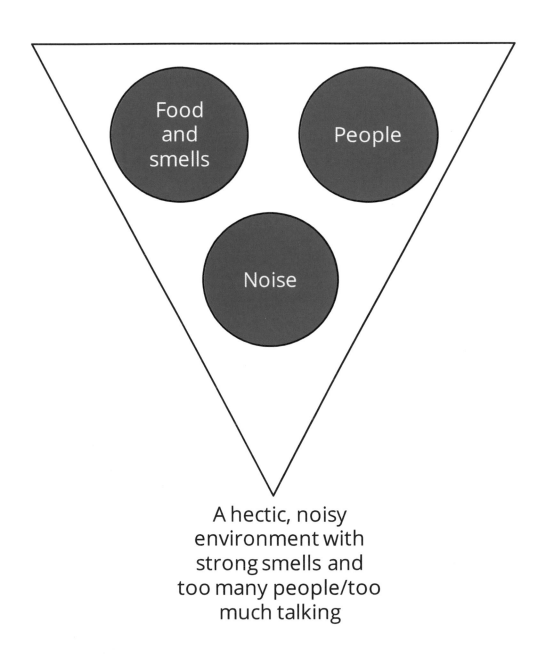

Food and smells

People

Noise

A hectic, noisy environment with strong smells and too many people/too much talking

Strategies for neurotypical siblings on coping with meltdowns

It can be helpful to teach your NT child anything they can do to help their ASD brother or sister when they sense a meltdown is looming. Some examples are shown here

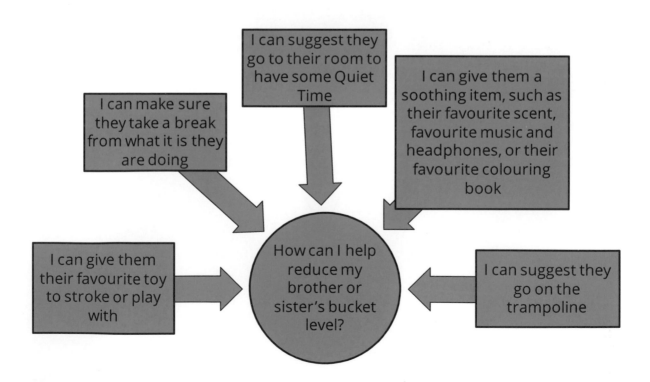

I can suggest they go to their room to have some Quiet Time

I can make sure they take a break from what it is they are doing

I can give them a soothing item, such as their favourite scent, favourite music and headphones, or their favourite colouring book

I can give them their favourite toy to stroke or play with

How can I help reduce my brother or sister's bucket level?

I can suggest they go on the trampoline

Helping your NT child to recognise the signs that their ASD brother or sister's bucket is getting full is a really good idea. The signs will be different for everyone, some examples are shown here

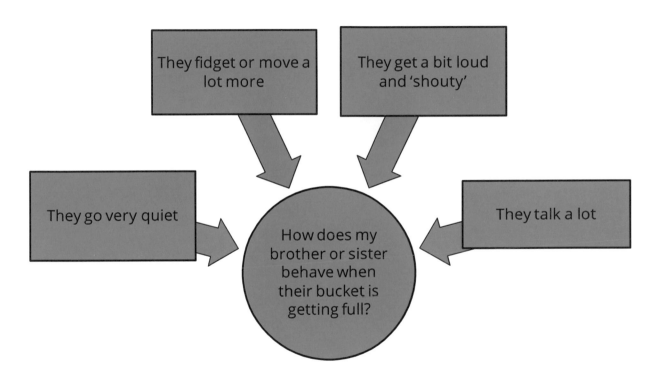

Then they could learn to tell their parents who can resolve the situation

Helping your NT child to recognise what sort of situations might cause their ASD brother or sister's bucket to get full is also a good idea

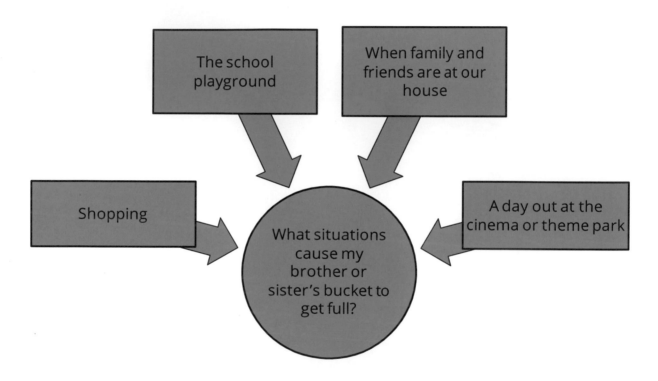

The school playground

When family and friends are at our house

Shopping

A day out at the cinema or theme park

What situations cause my brother or sister's bucket to get full?

Understanding the NT child's point of view during meltdowns

It is important to recognise how your NT child might feel about meltdowns and ensure they know what to do when they happen and where they can go to feel safe

Insecurity	
•due to not knowing how to act around their ASD sibling •due to not knowing how to react when a meltdown occurs	
Fear	
•of making the situation worse •of contributing to the bucket or the volcano	
Fright	
of getting physically hurt during the meltdown	
Fight	
wanting to 'attack' their ASD sibling	

Agree some rules as a family on what the NT child can do when a meltdown is happening

Make sure they always know that they should tell a parent or teacher

It's important for the NT child to understand that their brother or sister's meltdown is not their responsibility to manage

Communication

A lot of frustration between siblings can occur because of communication and misunderstandings

The NT child needs to learn that their ASD brother or sister is likely to require adaptations to the way they communicate with them

Some tips for good communication might be:

- Get their attention before speaking
- Allow them to finish what they are doing before speaking
- Use very clear, direct language
- Understand that when the ASD child asks "why?" or "what do you mean?", they're probably not being deliberately annoying, they most likely genuinely don't understand
- Using pictures, drawing or writing rather than talking
- Using choices rather than open ended questions
- Be aware of the environment - is it busy or noisy? This can make communicating very hard
- Be patient

Helpful: allowing *the autistic child* to finish what they are doing before you speak

Unhelpful: Using unclear, indirect language

Helpful: using very clear, direct language

Helpful: responding to "what do you mean?"

Unhelpful: responding to "what do you mean?"

Using open ended questions (less helpful) versus direct questions (more helpful)

Unhelpful: not getting their attention before speaking

Helpful: getting their attention before speaking

Alone Time

Make sure all family members know that it's important the ASD child has a large amount of Alone Time

Emphasise the importance of physical space, a calm environment, and personal belongings

Try to ensure that the NT sibling respects these needs

Summary

Neurotypical siblings of autistic children can find life extremely hard and their needs and feelings are sometimes overlooked

It's very important that their needs and feelings are addressed and that they get plenty of attention from their parents and spend time with their own friends

Neurotypical siblings will benefit from learning in particular to understand anxiety, meltdowns, sensory discomfort and Alone Time, and why their autistic brother or sister seems to get more of their parents' attention than they do

They will also benefit from learning how to more effectively communicate with their autistic brother or sister

Neurotypical and autistic siblings can have a really lovely relationship so long as there is some empathy and understanding from them both!

Many thanks for reading

Other books in The Visual Guides series at the time of writing:

Asperger's Syndrome (1)
Asperger's Syndrome: Meltdowns and Shutdowns
Asperger's Syndrome in 5-8 Year Olds
Asperger's Syndrome in 8-11 Year Olds
Asperger's Syndrome in 13-16 Year Olds
Asperger's Syndrome in 16-18 Year Olds
Asperger's Syndrome and Anxiety
Asperger's Syndrome: Socialising & Social Energy
Asperger's Syndrome and Puberty
Asperger's Syndrome: Meltdowns and Shutdowns (2)
Adapting Health Therapies for People on the Autism Spectrum
Asperger's Syndrome and Emotions
Asperger's Syndrome and Communication
Asperger's Syndrome and Executive Function
Asperger's Syndrome: Understanding Each Other (For ASD/NT Couples)

New titles are continually being produced so keep an eye out!

Printed in Poland
by Amazon Fulfillment
Poland Sp. z o.o., Wrocław